Tudor Medicine

Richard Tames

An imprint of Hodder Children's Books

The History Detective series
Tudor Home
Tudor Medicine
Tudor Theatre
Tudor War
Victorian Crime
Victorian Factory
Victorian School
Victorian Transport

First published in Great Britain in 2002 by Hodder Wayland, an imprint of Hodder Children's Books

Hodder Children's Books
A division of Hodder Headline Limited
338 Euston Road, London NW1 3BH

Editor: Kay Barnham
Designer: Simon Borrough
Cartoon artwork: Richard Hook
Picture research: Shelley Noronha – Glass Onion Pictures

British Library Cataloguing in Publication Data

Tames, Richard, 1946-
The history detective investigates Tudor medicine
1. Medicine – England – History – 16th century – Juvenile literature
2. England – Social conditions – 16th century – Juvenile literature
I. Title II. Tudor medicine
610.9'42'09031

ISBN 0 7502 3745 7

Printed and bound in Hong Kong

Picture acknowledgements:
The publishers would like to thank the following for permission to reproduce their pictures: The Bridgeman Art Library 15 (Ashmolean Museum, Oxford); 5 (Christie's Images); 18 (right) (National Portrait Gallery); 4 (top) (Rafael Valls Gallery, London); 7 (top and bottom), 9 (left) and *cover*, 10, 18 (left), 19, 21, 23 (top), 24 (right), 26, 27 (right) and *cover*; 4 (bottom), 11 (top), 14 (The Stapleton Collection); The Fotomas Index 20 (right), 22; Hodder Wayland Picture Library 16, 23 (bottom), 27 (left); Mary Evans Picture Library 1, 6, 8 and *cover*, 9 (right), 13 (top and bottom), 20 (left), 24 (bottom) and *cover*; Philip Sauvain Picture Collection 17, 25 (top); Science Museum/Science & Society Picture Library 12, 28 (top, bottom and *cover*), 29 and *cover*; The Wellcome Trust 11 (bottom).

Contents

Was it easy to survive in Tudor times?

The history detective Sherlock Bones, will help you to find clues and collect evidence about Tudor medicine – how doctors treated their patients and what medicine they used. Wherever you see one of Sherlock's paw-prints, you will find a mystery to solve. The answers can be found on pages 30 and 31.

Why do you think it was more dangerous to live in a town than in the countryside?

The Tudor family of kings and queens ruled England and Wales from 1485 to 1603. This was a time when medicine was still primitive, even for the few who could afford it. Tudors struggled to survive childbirth, violence, accidents and epidemics – and death rates were high.

During the summer months, outbreaks of diseases such as typhus or smallpox were common, with the plague also claiming many lives. Deaths were much higher in towns than in the countryside, so many well-off families moved to the countryside for the summer – where it was safer.

Murder was much more common than today. Most Tudor men carried a weapon to protect themselves, especially when travelling.

The rich Tudors below are fleeing from the plague.

Childbirth was a dangerous business. Women risked death at every birth – from blood loss, infection or the baby being in the wrong position. About one in sixteen births killed the mother and one in five babies died before the age of one.

This Tudor mother and baby were lucky enough to survive childbirth.

Tudors believed in Christianity, which taught that early or sudden death could be God's punishment for being wicked. Most people were also superstitious, believing that witchcraft could cause illness or accidents. Without science to explain sudden death, religion and superstition filled the gap.

DETECTIVE WORK

How long do men and women expect to live in Britain today? The death announcements in your local paper might give you some clues.

What sort of doctors were there?

The top doctors – who had usually studied at university – were called physicians. They were the only doctors who treated illnesses inside the body, such as stomach ulcers, and prescribed medicines to be swallowed. There were less than a thousand physicians in the whole of Tudor Britain, so their fees were very high. A visit from a physician could cost as much as a month's wages.

There were other types of doctor in Tudor times. Surgeons performed operations and treated external problems such as sores and rashes. As well as cutting hair, barbers also did minor surgery, including pulling teeth. In 1540, the two trades joined together as the College of Barber-Surgeons in London.

DETECTIVE WORK

Visit the websites for the Royal College of Physicians and the Royal College of Surgeons of Edinburgh. Their addresses can be found on page 31. Which college is older?

Henry VIII gave barber-surgeons like those above the right to dissect (cut up) the bodies of executed criminals for teaching purposes.

Do you think it was a good or a bad idea to learn medicine from the bodies of executed criminals?

Midwives helped women to give birth. They had no training or qualifications, but might have a church licence to show their experience and honesty. They were usually older women with children of their own.

Travelling doctors were quite common. Some were genuine, specializing in a particular skill, such as cutting stones from the bladder. But many were fakes, known as 'mountebanks' or 'quacks'. They charged to cure illnesses, often leaving before their patients found out they had been cheated.

A Tudor quack performing in front of an eager crowd.

Sir Hugh Platt had words of warning for people visiting barbers:

'... I am enforced to admonish all men to be careful how they suffer their teeth to be made white with any Aqua fortis (strong water) which is the Barber's usual water, for unless the same be... carefully applied, a man... may be driven to borrow a rank of teeth to eat his dinner with...'

The Jewel House of Art and Nature (1594)

Apothecaries mixed medicines and sold them from their shops.

What were the dangers of visiting the barber, according to Sir Hugh Platt (see above left)?

How were doctors trained?

Physicians learned Greek and Latin so that they could read the medical books by ancient Greek and Roman healers. The most famous of these was Claudius Galen (AD129–199). Galen was a Greek who lived in Rome and learned about medicine by patching up wounded gladiators.

Galen's idea of good health was based on the idea that the body was filled with four different 'humours' or fluids. If the body's fluids were unbalanced, illness was the result. The physician's job was to restore balance by making the patient sweat, vomit or go to the toilet. He might also change the patient's diet or drain off blood.

DETECTIVE WORK

Find out about the four humours (fluids) that doctors used to think were contained in the human body. The library and the Internet will help.

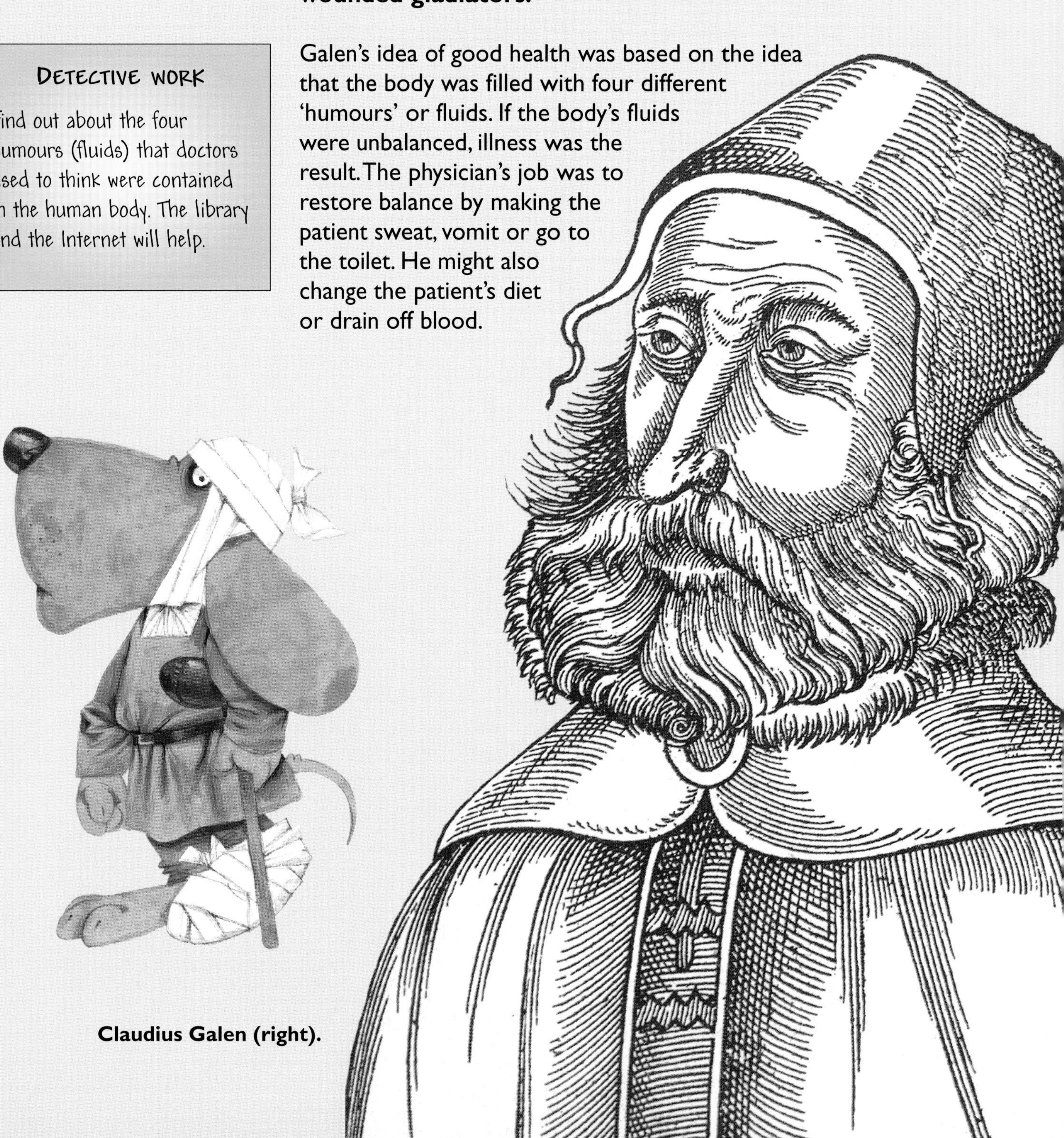

Claudius Galen (right).

Why do you think that the Church disapproved of dissection?

One Tudor doctor said that practising medicine was just as important as reading about it:

'... thou shalt never perfectly digest to thine own use any thing... except... that which thou hast seen before thine eyes and in the practice of thine own hands...'

Dr John Hall (1622)

Andreas Vesalius.

Physicians usually studied at Oxford or Cambridge University. Many of the best doctors studied abroad, at Padua in Italy or Montpellier in France. The most advanced teachers, such as Andreas Vesalius (1514–64), dissected bodies to find out how they worked. This greatly improved physicians' knowledge, but the Church disapproved.

Surgeons often learned how to perform operations by treating soldiers' illnesses and wounds. Many leading doctors trained with military or naval forces – like William Clowes (1540–1604) and Thomas Gale (1507–87) who both became royal physicians.

What wouldn't a doctor learn if he just treated Tudor soldiers?

Mary, Queen of Scots, gave Scottish barber-surgeons the right not to serve as soldiers, so long as they served instead as doctors.

How were medicines made?

Why do you think people used everyday items to make medicines?

Detective work

Search the Internet to find out why modern doctors think spiders' webs might be useful in medicine.

Tudor medicines were usually freshly made each time they were needed. Simple medicines were based on plants or household items such as ale, milk or honey. However, Dr John Hall used over a hundred different ingredients in his medicines, including herbs, pigeons' livers, chicken droppings and spiders' webs.

Medicines were used to relieve pain, make people go to the toilet or make them sleep. Some medicines were supposed to restore unbalanced humours (see page 8) by making the patient vomit or sweat. Wearing heavy clothes made of linen, wool or leather that were rarely washed meant people got fleas or lice. They needed home-made lotions to kill vermin and soothe insect bites.

Herbs and plants were grown in this Tudor garden especially for use in medicines.

Andrew Boorde, an important Tudor physician, wrote of his cure for sleeplessness:

'Take of the oil of violets an ounce, of opium half an ounce, incorporate this together with woman's milk and with a fine linen cloth lay it to the temples...'

Breviary of Health (1547)

Herbs were often used for healing. Many Tudors knew how to use them to make medicines, but herbalists were the experts. They knew when and where to gather each plant at its best and whether to use the roots, stem, leaves, flower or seeds. Tudor herbalists would then turn their ingredients into powders, pills, plasters, potions and ointments.

What problems might there be in using herbs for medicines?

During Tudor times, doctors began testing different medicine ingredients one at a time to watch their effects. A Swiss doctor, Paracelsus (1493–1541), introduced medicines based on chemicals, not herbs.

Ceres
Pomona
Exciderat ne tibi diuini muneris Author:
Præsentem monstrat quælibet herba Deum.
THE
HERBALL
OR GENERALL
Historie of
Plantes.
Gathered by John Gerarde
of London Master in
CHIRVRGERIE
Very much
Enlarged and Amended by
Thomas Johnson
Citizen and Apothecarye
of
LONDON.
London Printed by
Adam Islip Joice Norton
and Richard Whitakers
Anno 1633.

John Gerard was a famous Tudor herbalist. The title page of his book – *The Herball* – is shown above.

The first person to use chemicals in medicines in Tudor Britain was William Butler (left).

Did the Tudors perform operations?

Physicians performed simple operations such as setting broken bones, but surgery was a last resort. Today, patients are given anaesthetics to make them unconscious. In Tudor times, patients were wide awake. They often died of pain and shock during an operation, so surgeons had to be fast. The best could cut off, or amputate, a leg in under a minute.

A good saw was needed to amputate an arm or leg.

Without antiseptics to fight germs, patients who survived surgery often died of infection afterwards. If there was major damage inside the body, or to the head, the patient faced almost certain death.

Tudor battlefields brought new challenges for Tudor surgeons. Gunshots destroyed flesh and muscle, shattering bone into fragments and forcing dirty clothing into wounds, causing infection.

The leading expert on gunshot wounds, John of Vigo, believed that gunpowder itself was poisonous. He recommended that wounds should be cleaned with boiling oil. Unfortunately, this often killed the patient.

In 1536 a young French doctor, Ambrose Paré (1509–90), treating soldiers after a battle, ran out of oil and made up a cool dressing instead. He discovered this worked much better than boiling oil. He later used an ointment of ground-up earthworms mixed with puppy fat to treat wounds.

Ambrose Paré described how difficult it was to amputate:

'... who can without pain cut off an arm or leg...? A surgeon must have a strong, stable and fearless hand and a mind determined and merciless... as if he were nothing affected by their cries...'

Ambrose Paré.

What instruments do you think the doctor below would have used to cut off the soldier's leg?

Paré amputates a soldier's leg on the battlefield.

Were there female doctors?

Before the Colleges of Physicians and Barber-Surgeons began to organize medical training and treatment, most people relied on their families to heal them. But, as the teaching of medicine became more official, with years of study and examinations, women found it more and more difficult to become doctors. As girls did not go to school and learn Latin, they could not go to university to study medicine.

Do you think the women in the picture below were trained in midwifery?

However, many noble-women were taught how to read and write at home and then learned how to make medicines for their family and neighbours. One of Lady Grace Mildmay's (1552–1620) medicines contained 169 ingredients and was made up in batches of 10 gallons (47 litres). Lady Margaret Hoby (1571–1633) even did minor surgery.

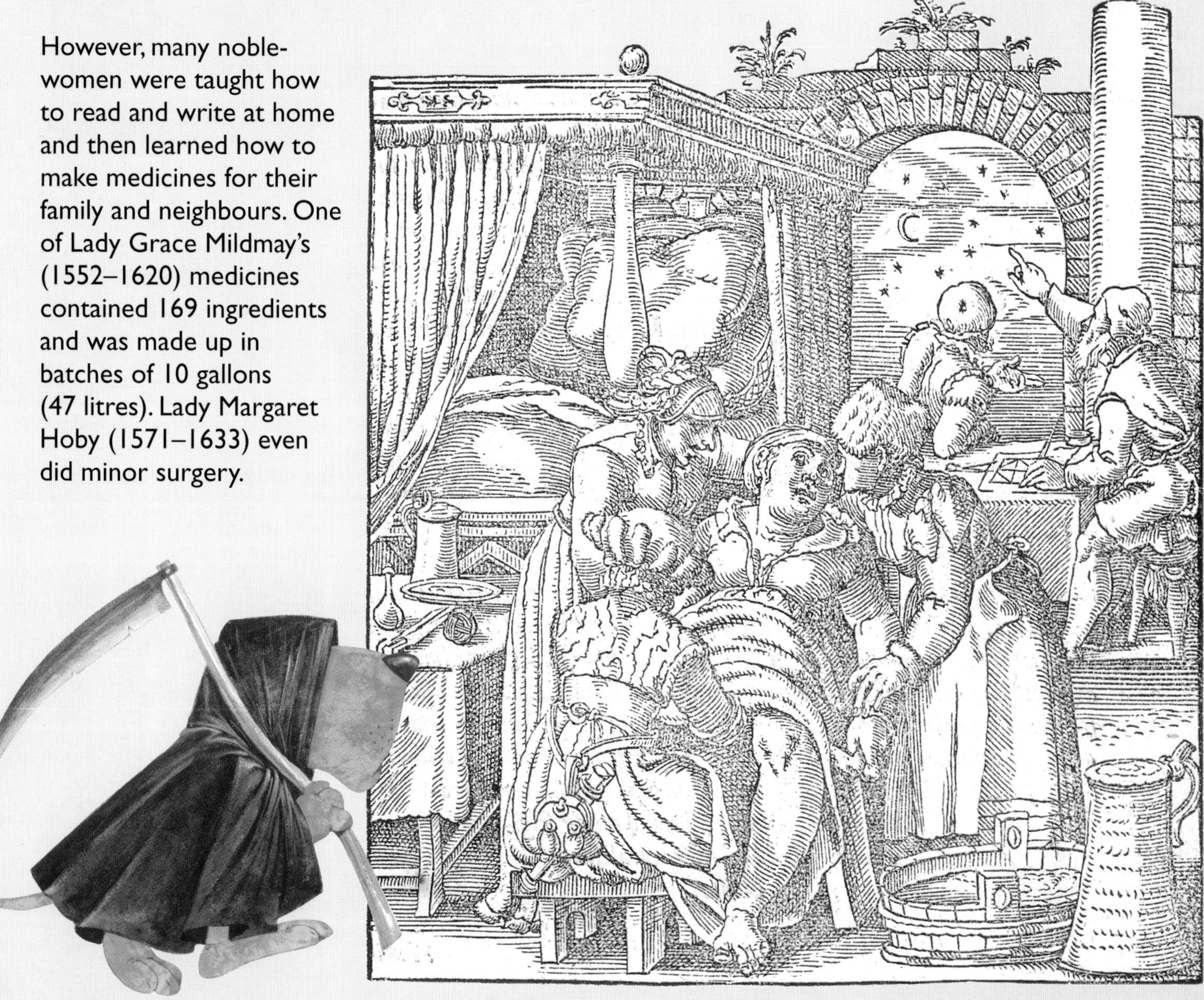

Midwifery was an area of medicine usually left to women.

Tudor people thought that a 'wise woman' or 'white witch' would have a kitchen like this.

Apart from midwives, many villages had 'wise women' or 'white witches' who made up medicines. Some really were skilled healers but others pretended to be able to use magic. Many of both sorts became victims of the 'witchcraft craze', which came to a peak around 1580-1600. Sudden illness in a healthy person and mental illness were often blamed on witchcraft because people could not explain them otherwise.

'As the killing witch must die, the healing and harmless witch must die... though he kill not... by witches we understand not only those which kill and torment but all diviners, all wizards... commonly called wise men and wise women... and in the same number we reckon all good witches, which do no hurt but good, which do not spoil and destroy but save and deliver...'

William Perkins, *A Discourse of the Damned Art of Witchcraft* (1608)

Detective work

Use your local library to find out about people who were accused of witchcraft in the sixteenth or seventeenth centuries. How did people think witches could be identified?

Were there hospitals?

In 1500, there were hundreds of monasteries and nunneries in Britain. The monks and nuns who lived in them cared for the sick and took in orphans and old people. However, in the 1530s, Henry VIII abolished the monasteries, and took away their wealth and lands.

Doctors are making the most of the space available in this hospital ward.

Later in Tudor times, three former religious institutions were refounded in London. These were St Thomas's, St Bartholomew's and Bethlehem, Britain's only hospital for the treatment of mental illness. Many leading physicians served on the staff of these hospitals. One of these physicians was William Harvey (1578–1657) of St Bartholomew's. He made the discovery that blood circulates around the human body.

Detective work

St Bartholomew's (also known as 'Bart's') and St Thomas's still exist. Use the library and the Internet to find out more about the history of these famous hospitals.

Special hospitals called 'lazar-houses' looked after people suffering from leprosy. As leprosy died out, the lazar-houses took in people with other skin diseases and with illnesses that could not be cured.

During epidemics, many towns also set up temporary pest-houses, where the sick could go to die. In this way, they hoped to keep infection under control. Some surgeons took patients into their own houses so that they could aid their recovery. Otherwise they put them in lodgings nearby.

One Tudor physician thought that mentally ill patients should be treated in this harsh way:

'... every man the which is mad... to be kept in safeguard, in some close house or chamber, where there is little light. And that he have a keeper the which the mad man do fear... Also the chamber... that the mad man is in, let there be no painted cloths, nor painted walls, nor pictures... for such things make them full of fantasies. And use few words to them...'

Andrew Boorde (1567)

A lazar-house in Oxford.

Who treated royalty?

Royal physicians looked after the health of Tudor royals. It was up to the physicians to make sure that the kings and queens were not poisoned. They also treated any illnesses and attended the births of royal children. In return they were honoured and highly paid. The medical history of Tudor rulers suggests, however, that even the most expensive treatment was often useless.

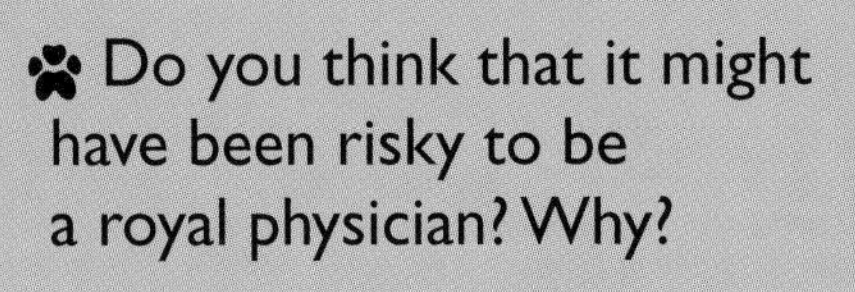

Do you think that it might have been risky to be a royal physician? Why?

William Butts was one of Henry VIII's personal physicians.

This painting shows Henry VIII on his deathbed, pointing to his son and heir, Edward VI.

It is doubtful whether Henry VIII's doctors helped him. The Tudor king was very fit when he was young, but later, he suffered from gout – a very painful disease. Henry loved red meat and wine, which probably made his gout worse. When he was 50 his legs were so swollen he could hardly walk.

Royal doctors were also unable to save Jane Seymour, Henry VIII's favourite wife. Queen Jane died after giving birth to Henry's

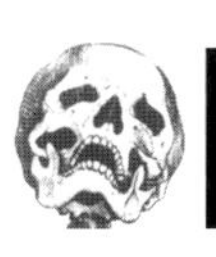

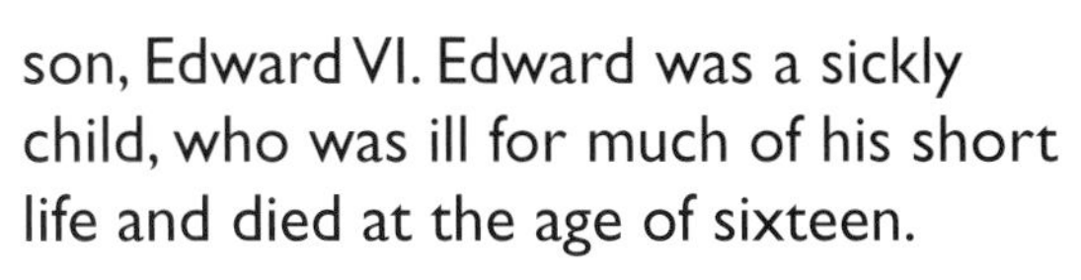

son, Edward VI. Edward was a sickly child, who was ill for much of his short life and died at the age of sixteen.

Queen Mary, Henry VIII's daughter, was desperate to have a son. When her stomach finally began to grow larger, she was overjoyed. Sadly, Mary was not pregnant, but suffering from cancer. This led to her death.

Mary's doctor probably knew she was not pregnant, but did not dare say anything. Why do you think this was?

Mary Tudor was the eldest of King Henry VIII's children.

'In the very end of May, began in the city of London... the sweating sickness... The King was sore troubled for divers [several] died in the court... so that the King for a space removed almost every day, till at the last he came to... a place of the Abbot of St Alban's... which place was so purged [cleaned] daily with fires... that... none of their company was infected...'

Edward Hall –
Life of Henry VIII (1548)

DETECTIVE WORK

Search on the Internet to find out why Roderigo Lopez was hanged and quartered at Tyburn in 1594.

What kinds of medical books were there?

Before the invention of printing, books were handwritten – and very expensive. A handwritten Bible took three years to copy, but a printed book the same size could be produced ninety times faster and ten times cheaper. As printing spread through Europe, more and more books were translated from Latin so that ordinary people could read them in their own language.

A fifteenth-century printer's workshop would have looked like this.

❦ Why do you think newly printed pages were hung up?

Doctors improved their reputations and their incomes by writing books. Some wrote reference books and textbooks for other doctors to use. There were also general books for the public, containing advice about healthy living. Sir Thomas Elyot (1490–1546), a courtier, outraged doctors by writing a medical handbook in English, called *The Castle of Health*. But, by the time Elizabeth I died in 1603, over 150 medical books had been published in English.

Andrew Boorde, one of Henry VIII's physicians, wrote a book which included prescriptions to cure baldness and failing eyesight.

DETECTIVE WORK

Find out about more famous Tudor medical books from the websites of the British Library and the Wellcome Foundation for the History of Medicine.

Most health handbooks emphasized the importance of diet, exercise and a healthy environment. Idleness, over-eating and worry were seen as being dangerous to health. Riding, dancing and tennis were recommended for exercise. The fact that these were pastimes for the rich shows that the writers of health handbooks were not very interested in the health of the poor.

'Real tennis' was a sport enjoyed by rich Tudors.

Why do you think medical writers were interested in the health of rich, not poor, Tudors?

In his 1607 poem, Sir John Harrington wrote of the benefits of garlic. Garlic is still seen as a healthy food.

'Since Garlic then hath power to save from death;
Bear with it though it make unsavoury breath;
And scorn not Garlic like to some, that think
It only makes men wink and drink and stink.'

Was there medical help for the poor?

The poor suffered from illness more than the wealthy. There were many reasons for this. Poor Tudors often ate food that was going bad and lived in overcrowded rooms in filthy slums. Many worked in dirty or dangerous jobs, risking infection, cuts or burns.

DETECTIVE WORK

Find out what the Poor Law was and how it worked in your local area.

Local government was run by magistrates known as Justices of the Peace (JPs). They divided the poor into 'deserving' and 'undeserving'. Undeserving poor were those who refused to work, although they were fit and well. Deserving poor were unable to work because they were too old, disabled or sick. JPs thought these poor people deserved help for two reasons. Firstly, caring for the poor was a religious duty. Secondly, if the sick poor were cured, they could go back to work.

Well-run cities often paid a doctor to take care of the poor. Even so, the poor might be forced to sell almost everything they owned before they qualified as being poor enough for free treatment.

Justices of the Peace decided whether the poor deserved help or not.

A Tudor beggar is whipped through the streets.

Thomas Tusser wrote of the ways in which a wife could prevent sickness in her husband:

'Good housewives provide,
ere a sickness do come,
Of sundry good things in her
house to have some...
Cold herbs in her garden for
agues that burn,
That over-strong heat to good
temper may turn...
Good broth and good keeping,
do much now and then,
Good diet with wisdom, best
comforteth men.'

The Points of Housewifery United to the Comfort of Husbandrie (1570)

A few doctors charged rich patients high fees, while treating the poor for nothing. Sometimes, JPs gave poor people licences to beg from door to door until they had collected enough to pay for their treatment. Incurables might be sent to the lazar-house, where they would be fed and cared for. Undeserving poor lived by begging or stealing. Some JPs thought they ought to be whipped and branded and sent on their way.

Why do you think that beggars were branded?

A nobleman ignores a beggar.

How did the Tudors fight plagues?

The Black Death of 1347–9 was a worldwide outbreak of bubonic plague. It was carried aboard trading ships from Asia to Europe, where a third of all people died. Beggars and gypsies were blamed for spreading the plague, but it was actually carried by the fleas living on rats.

There were many outbreaks of the plague in London, before, during and after Tudor times. Bristol had an outbreak in 1575 and Norwich suffered in 1579, 1585 and 1592. The plague usually began in the poorest, dirtiest, most crowded areas of a city.

The plague struck suddenly, spread rapidly and was nearly always fatal. It was horribly painful. Most sufferers developed buboes – hard, pus-filled boils in the groin and armpits. Lancing them to let out the pus caused even more pain.

When the plague broke out, the only sensible thing to do was to run away. Most physicians did. A few doctors stayed to help the sick, but some of their treatments – for example, rubbing sores with salt and vinegar or burning them with hot irons – only made the patient worse. Most doctors tending the sick died themselves.

The Diſeaſes and Caſualties this Week.

ABortive	6
Aged	54
Apoplexie	1
Bedridden	1
Cancer	2
Childbed	23
Chriſomes	15
Collick	1
Conſumption	174
Convulſion	88
Dropſie	40
Drownd two, one at St. Kath. Tower, and one at Lambeth	2
Feaver	353
Fiſtula	1
Flox and Small-pox	[illegible]
Flux	2
Found dead in the Street at St. Bartholomew the Leſs	1
Frighted	1
Gangrene	1
Gowt	1
Grief	1
Griping in the Guts	74
Jaundies	3
Impoſthume	18
Infants	21
Killed by a fall down ſtairs at St. Thomas Apoſtle	1

Kingſevil	10
Le[illegible]gy	1
Murthered at Stepney	1
P[illegible]lſie	2
Plague	3880
Pluriſie	1
Quinſie	6
Rickets	23
Riſing of the Lights	19
Rupture	2
Sciatica	1
Scowring	13
Scurvy	1
Sore legge	1
Spotted Feaver and Purples	190
Starved at Nurſe	1
Stilborn	8
Stone	2
Stopping of the ſtomach	16
Strangury	1
Suddenly	1
Surfeit	87
Teeth	113
Thruſh	3
Tiſſick	6
Ulcer	2
Vomiting	7
Winde	8
Wormes	18

Chriſtned: Males — 83, Females — 83, In all — 166. Buried: Males — 2656, Females — 2663, In all — 5319. Plague — 3880

Increaſed in the Burials this Week — 1289

Pariſhes clear of the Plague — 34 Pariſhes Infected — 96

The Aßize of Bread ſet forth by Order of the Lord Maior and Court of Aldermen

A penny Wheaten Loaf to contain Nine Ounces and a half, and three half-penny White Loaves the like weight

This almanac from 1665 shows how many people died in London in just one week.

Can you see how many people died from the plague in the record above?

This painting is called *Dance of Death*. This kind of painting reminded people that death could happen at any time. The artist showed both rich and poor people, because no one could escape…

One medical book advised poor people to coat plague sores with eggs, flour, honey and turpentine. Another suggested cutting a puppy in half and rubbing it over the sores.

Detective work

A well-known nursery rhyme is said to be about the plague. Can you find out which one?

This churchyard at Sandhurst in Kent is believed to be the site of a plague pit, where many plague victims were buried in one huge grave.

A city was not the place to be when the plague broke out:

'... all merry meetings are cut off... Playhouses stand... the doors locked up... like houses lately infected, from whence the affrighted dwellers are fled, in hope to live better in the country.'

Thomas Dekker (1609)

How can we find out about Tudor medicine?

DETECTIVE WORK
You can find out about surviving hospital records for your town or city on the following website:
http://hospitalrecords.pro.gov.uk
Which was the first hospital in your area?

Historians find out about Tudor medicine from the records kept by cities and hospitals. However, records tell how hospitals were run, rather than how patients were treated. The records of the College of Physicians or Colleges of Barber-Surgeons show how doctors were trained.

Tudor medical books show how doctors recognized illnesses and injuries and the treatments and medicines they suggested. These books explain how people thought medicine worked at that time.

This doctor is treating a patient who is suffering from gangrene.

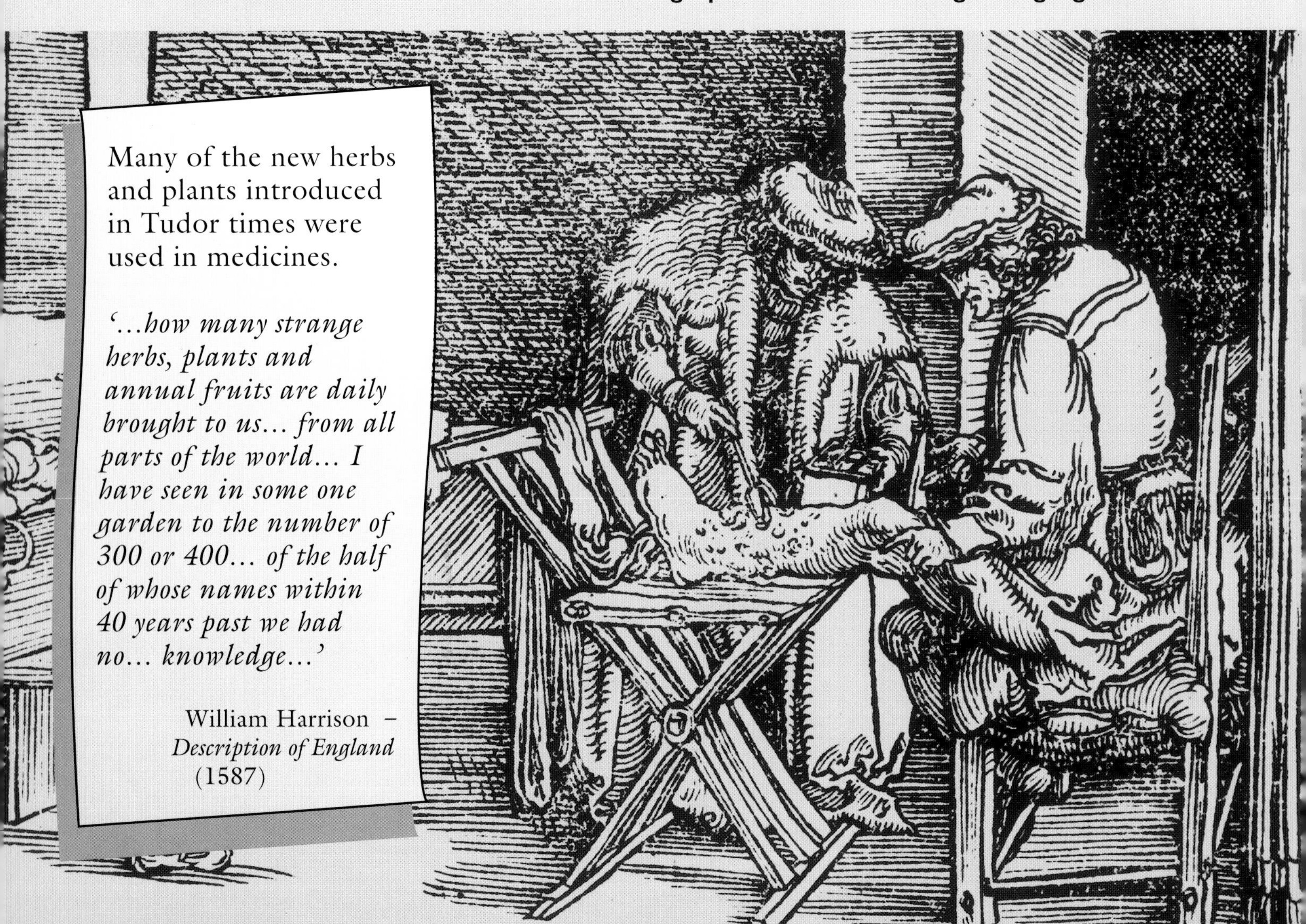

Many of the new herbs and plants introduced in Tudor times were used in medicines.

'...how many strange herbs, plants and annual fruits are daily brought to us... from all parts of the world... I have seen in some one garden to the number of 300 or 400... of the half of whose names within 40 years past we had no... knowledge...'

William Harrison – *Description of England* (1587)

Detective work
You can find out more about skeletons if you search for London Bodies at the Museum of London website (see page 31).

Letters and diaries tell us how things seemed from the patient's view. Families often kept books of recipes for food, perfumes, make-up and medicines, all mixed up together. Letters between friends confirm that Tudor people worried about illness a lot.

Skeletons can show signs of death caused by violence, surgical operations, bone disease or poor diet.

Many Tudors had very good teeth because sugar was too rare to cause tooth decay.
Tooth enamel can show how well an adult ate as a child and whether they suffered from a serious illness.

A museum expert checks a human skull for evidence of disease.

Your project

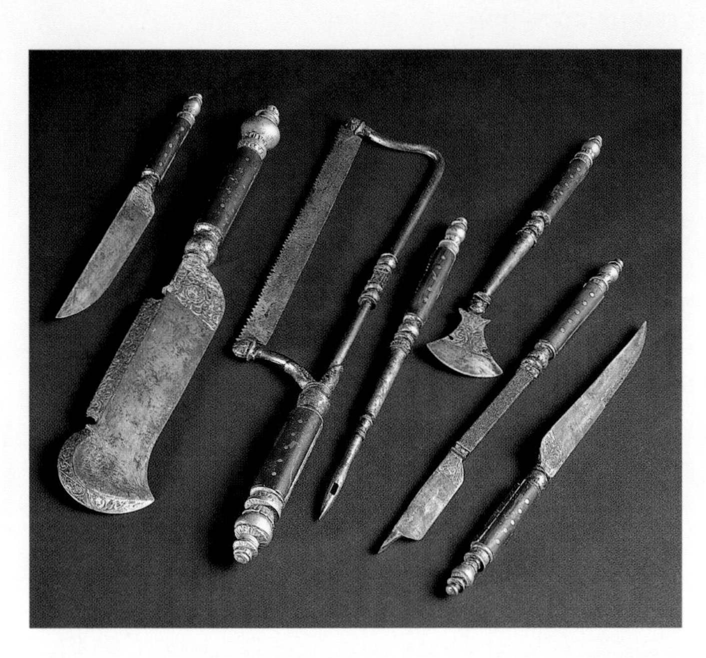

Have you followed the detective work activities in this book? If so, you should now be able to track down enough clues to produce your own project about Tudor medicine. First, decide on a topic to investigate. Choose something that you find really interesting – or really gruesome! You could get some ideas by looking through this book's index. You could also use one of the questions on page 29 as a starting point.

Sixteenth-century surgical instruments.

Topic Questions

- Can you describe the career of a typical Tudor doctor?
- What do we know about illness and its treatment in Tudor times?
- Can you describe a visit to a hospital in Tudor times?
- If you could interview a top Tudor doctor what would you ask?
- Do people use herbs to treat illness nowadays?

Project Presentation

- Write an advertisement for a new handbook of medicine you are publishing for English families in 1600. Your advertisement should include a table of contents and a note about the author and his qualifications for writing the book.
- Assemble your own Tudor medicine chest (e.g. rosemary, garlic and honey). Write a handbook of instructions for their use.
- Draw up a contract of employment setting out the duties of a physician you have hired to treat the poor in your town.
- Write a diary recording how an outbreak of plague in a village might have been observed by its vicar.

Sherlock Bones has been finding out about whether there were vets – doctors for animals – in Tudor times. He has discovered that there were special doctors for horses called farriers. Lots of books were written about how to cure horses' diseases and injuries. Horses were used for travelling, hunting, warfare and pulling carts and ploughs, so they were very valuable. Sherlock was pleased to find that people were also interested in keeping dogs healthy – but only if they were used for hunting. He was surprised to learn that Tudors didn't care much about cats and other animals!

Students watching a doctor dissect a body.

Glossary

ague An illness involving fever and shivering.
amputate Cut off a limb.
archive A collection of historic documents and records.
dressing A bandage.
epidemic Widespread outbreak of a disease.
gangrene When part of a body starts to die.
gladiator A man in ancient Rome trained to fight against other men or animals.
gout A disease which causes arthritis, usually in the feet and legs.
leprosy A disease which attacks the skin and nerves.
lice Tiny insects that can live on humans, causing itching.
ointment Medicine that is rubbed on to a sore place on the body.
operation When a patient has medical treatment, especially cutting them open to repair something inside their body.
patient A person who is ill.
physician A type of doctor.
plague A killer infection carried by rat fleas.
primitive A very early version of something.
smallpox A dangerous disease caused by a virus; often fatal, usually causing scarring of the skin.
sore A painful place on the body.
superstitious Believing that certain things will bring good or bad luck.
surgeon A doctor who performs surgery.
surgery When an operation is performed.
treatment Looking after a patient to try and make them well again.
typhus A disease spread by fleas, causing fever and a rash; often fatal.
ulcers Open sores, either on the skin or inside the body.
vermin Animals or insects that harm other living things, such as rats, fleas, lice.

Answers

page 4
- Townsfolk were more crowded together, without proper drains or waste disposal, so infections spread faster. Country people usually had fresher food and cleaner water.

page 6
- Good – they could learn some basic anatomy. Bad – death by execution wouldn't tell anything about death by disease. Because most executed criminals were grown men there was little chance to learn about females or children.

page 7
- A trip to the barber could be dangerous because some of their treatments might make your teeth fall out!

page 9
- A doctor who just treated Tudor soldiers would not learn about illnesses affecting women, children and the elderly.
- It was believed that when the world ended the dead would be brought back to life; the Church believed that the dead had to be buried whole, in order for them to live again.

page 10
- Everyday items such as herbs were available, had some medical value and the poor could not afford anything else.

page 11
- People might use herbs that were too old to work, confuse them with other herbs, use the wrong part or use the wrong quantity.

page 13
- The doctor would need a sharp knife (scalpel) to cut through skin, muscle and other tissue. Then he would use a saw to cut through the bone.

page 14
🐾 The midwives in the picture would not have as much experience of different kinds of birth problems as someone working full time.

page 18
🐾 A royal physician might be suspected of wanting to harm the ruler and punished if he failed to cure the king or queen.

page 19
🐾 It was less risky to keep silent until the queen herself realized she was not pregnant but ill and needed her doctor's help.

page 20
🐾 The sheets of paper were hung up until the ink was dry, so that it didn't smudge.

page 21
🐾 Poor people could not afford to pay for treatment, so doctors would make no money out of them.

page 23
🐾 Beggars were branded to warn others what they were.

page 24
🐾 The record shows that 3880 people died from the plague in just one week.

Books to read

The Tudor Remedy Book
by Nicholas Culpeper (A & C Black, 1990)

Look Inside: A Tudor Medicine Chest
by Brian Moses (Hodder Wayland, 1999)

Places to visit

You can visit the home of Shakespeare's son-in-law, Dr John Hall.

Hall's Croft
Old Town
Stratford-upon-Avon
Warwickshire
Tel: (01789) 292107
http://www.Stratford.co.uk/birthplace/home

Websites

The Time Traveller's Guide to Tudor England
http://www.channel4.com/history/microsites/H/history/guide16/hazardsx.html

The Museum of London website
http://www.museum-london.org./uk

The Royal College of Physicians
www.rcplondon.ac.uk/college/about_history

The Royal College of Surgeons, Edinburgh
www.rcsed.ac.uk/geninfo/ history/

Index

Numbers in **bold** refer to pictures and captions.

DA